Spot the Difference Grammar
Level 1
Amber Domoradzki

Copyright © 2024 by Amber Domoradzki

All right reserved.

Mention of specific companies, organizations, or authorities in this book does not imply explicit endorsement by the author, nor does mention of specific companies, organizations, or authorities imply that they endorse this book.

All internet addresses were current at the time of publication.

Dedication

This book is for Henry, the rambunctious little boy who helped me see the value in Spot the Difference Grammar.

Table of Contents

Welcome to Spot the Difference Grammar Level 1! 7
Benefits of Spot the Difference Grammar 15
Quick tips for getting started 16
Recommended children's books 17
Thank you! 18
Section 1 Spelling and Letter Recognition 19
Section 2 Punctuation and Capitalization 37
Section 3 Parts of Speech 83
Section 4 Review 135

Welcome to Spot the Difference Grammar Level 1!

Hello and welcome!

Most of us are familiar with how much children love to spot the differences between two pictures, such as they do in the popular children's activity found on many worksheets. In Spot the Difference Grammar, children do this, except that they find the differences between two sets of sentences, one that is grammatically correct and another that is incorrect. While doing something that they notoriously love doing, kids can also learn a bit of grammar!

I thought of Spot the Difference Grammar while doing an activity with my kids where we edited a paragraph. As it put grammar in context, I thought it was a great activity. However, how would students be able to identify what was correct before being shown what was incorrect? I faced this same issue when I worked as a software test engineer. New hires would be asked to test a product before being shown what a passing test would look like. New hires, just like children new to the world of language syntax, need clear guidelines of what is correct before diving into figuring out what is incorrect. And, so, I thought of having side-by-side sentences for children to compare, one set that is correct and another that is incorrect. Spot the Difference Grammar was born.

Far from being gimmicky, spotting the differences between differently formatted sentences is great for helping children hone their grammar skills. What we call "good writing" is probably more appropriately called "good editing." Many if not most of us can write our thoughts down in a stream-of-conscious way. To make sure our writing is understandable to others, we have to go back and re-read what we wrote, looking for relatively minor things as we make sure that what we wrote is correct or, at least, what we intended to write. In other words, we have to edit what we wrote, by observing what we wrote in a plain, objective manner. Spot the Difference Grammar hones this skill. In this program, children are invited to observe writing, noticing relatively small—but important—details. Children can sit back in a relaxed way, without being bogged down by too many complicated things, like how to hold a pencil or write letters neatly, as they notice things about sentences. I personally found that this approach to learning made children feel very smart. I would watch as children would sit deep in thought while doing the exercises, perhaps bringing a pencil to their lips as they mulled over the differences in the sentences. One particularly rambunctious child told me, "I am going to *destroy* Spot the Difference Grammar!" Parents who have tried the program often tell me that their children take to the lessons right away and often want to do page after page. Some parents have told me that this was the only program that didn't frustrate their children. Yet other parents with language-gifted children said that their children enjoyed the program and wanted more differences to find and more activities to do. These activities, where children do something that is naturally fun to them, should be a confidence-inducing slam dunk for them. The idea is to empower children and make them feel "on top" of grammar, not that grammar is on top of them.

This program is also ideal for helping students appreciate the beauty of well-formatted sentences, i.e. the beauty and importance of grammar itself. In an ironic twist, by showing them incorrectly formatted sentences, we show students the need for formatting sentences correctly. It is a bit like Goldilocks and the Three Bears. Just as Goldilocks experiments with her "too hot" and "too cold" before getting to her "just right," in Spot the Difference Grammar students are shown what is just a bit off, as we guide them to what is "just right." In showing students sentences that are incorrectly formatted, we show them how poorly formatted sentences come across, which is hilariously wrong. When we remove a critical part of speech, for instance, it becomes clear that the sentence makes no sense. (I encourage you to read the incorrect sentences in a spirit of great fun!) In this simple, pressure-free program, students are gently nudged to see the beauty in correctly formatted sentences, which we do not to follow a set of blind rules but entirely for clarity and purpose.

As a home educator, I personally found that this is a great way to teach grammar: by asking children to simply observe sentences. However, I found that simply giving them a sentence and asking them, "What do you observe?" was simply too open-ended. In practice, I found they need more of a prompt than this. In Spot the Difference Grammar, on the other hand, there is a purpose to the activities and a built-in control of error: students are told there is a certain number of differences to find and they have succeeded when they have found all of them. There is a clear purpose, a strong control of error, and a definite lesson taught as students find the differences and then work through the supplemental activities.

The Observant Mom child development work

I made this grammar program for children, but what I am most known for is the child development work I do, which is used by tens of thousands around the world. I document the age-related "stages" children go through. These stages are those times children "act up" but on the other side of this period of disarray is new mental growth. I document both the "irritable" behavior and the new growth that comes after it. My work can be found at my website, The Observant Mom, www.theobservantmom.com.

This grammar program was not specifically inspired by the child development work I do, but it is in great alignment with what my work has found is the way children naturally learn. In doing my child development work, which documents notable child behavior on a nearly daily basis across years at a time, I noticed that children repeatedly went through predictable cycles of growth that lasted about 2-3 months at a time. These cycles start with children becoming deeply imaginative and end with them having a new practical skill set. I call this cycle a "hill" because children go "up" into fantasy and come back "down" to reality. Each hill has predictable sub-cycles, which are,

The stages of a "Hill" of child development

1. Imagination. At first children become deeply and wildly imaginative. They often imagine that they can do something that is impossible, and they often want to go find something.
2. Curiosity. After this imaginative stage, children get highly curious. This is one of their many "Why?" stages.
3. Clarity. Due to this curiosity, children develop a large databank of knowledge.
4. Creativity. With new knowledge, children get creative just to be creative.
5. Application. With this hands-on experience from their happy play, children then take initiative and apply their skills to real life situations.
6. Reflection. Finally, they become deeply self-reflective about what they just went through.

This Spot the Difference Grammar program greatly follows this natural learning cycle. First, in the deeply imaginative stage, children are often sparked to go find something or try something— often something near impossible! They want to see if they can jump across a river or shrink into a toy. They also want to go find things. This might explain why children love hide-and-seek games and Spot the Difference Grammar is a sort of hide-and-seek game. Second, in their "curious" sub-stage or rather one of their many "Why?" stages, I found children would naturally sort things in a "this is this" and "that is that" way. At this sub-stage, children often ask wild questions about the world such as, "What happens if I jump in the swimming pool with my clothes on?" This helps them sort something: clothes absorb water whereas bathing suits don't. Spot the Difference Grammar helps children sort things as they find the differences between the Correct and Incorrect set of sentences. These sentences are also hilariously "wrong," which is what sometimes children need to see first. Children seem to need to see things in a wrong way, as they bend, break, and test both things and ideas, as to gain an appreciation for the right way—what is stable, what is true. I think this might be why the story of Goldilocks and The Three Bears is a perennial favorite: children enjoy exploring what is wrong before settling on what is right.

Next, after the Curiosity stage, there is what I call a Clarity stage. After asking all sorts of questions about the world, children develop an impressive databank of knowledge. With clarity comes confidence and with confidence comes creativity. In the Creative stage, children use the information they have acquired in a creative way, playing just to play. After this, with a bit of experience under their belt, they then apply their knowledge to real-life situations as they arise. Finally, after they have gone up and over this "hill," children become deeply self-reflective. They often think that their former self, before they went through this cycle, was babyish. Children can get harsh and critical of themselves. But in it, they've developed tremendous confidence, new skills, and a new level of self-awareness.

The Spot the Difference and supplemental activities

In understanding this cycle of how children learn, as well as using my own experience in educating children, I thus added some supplementary activities to this program. Each lesson, which are numbered, consists of two pages. On the first page is the Spot the Difference activity. The two sets of sentences are marked as **Correct** and **Incorrect**. Students find the listed number of differences between these two sets of sentences. This mirrors children's "Imaginative" stage, where they like to find things.

Note that every use of a particular grammar concept in the spot the difference activities is "correct" or "incorrect." Some are stylistic choices. Choosing to italicize a word, for instance, is a stylistic choice. In these cases, I present them as "Option 1" and "Option 2," instead of as "Correct" and "Incorrect." I explain as much in the "Lesson" that follows the Spot the Difference activity.

The Lesson taught

On the second page of every lesson are the supplemental activities. The first thing is an explanation of the grammar concept just illustrated.

Word lists

In addition to an explanation of the grammar concept just illustrated, one thing I added in many of the supplemental exercises are simple words lists showing, for example, common plural nouns, common adjectives, etc. I found children simply like looking at such word lists. These word lists, which parents also tell me children enjoy looking through, follow along with the "Clarity" sub-stage that I just described, where children enjoy building a databank of knowledge, simply by reading or watching things that give them knowledge.

Sentence expansion activities

I also added, when appropriate, open-ended sentences that children could complete. I again simply found that children often liked doing this kind of sentence expansion activity. They might simply fill in, "The sun is _____." This follows along with the "Creative" sub-stage of the learning cycle described above. In this case, they can fill in the sentence with whatever they want. The sun is… yellow, big, hot, silly, whatever.

Note that I found many children enjoyed filling in these kinds of sentences. I, as such, filled up any given lesson with as many of these activities as I could fit in a page, at the behest of some parents who said their kids wanted more. However, I found that not all children want to fill in the sentences at these young ages. Some young children simply aren't into writing yet. For these children, I encourage you to let them fill in what they want and otherwise let them verbally state their answers.

Find or fix the error activities

I also added an exercise to nearly every lesson where students could *apply* their new skill. These are the exercises where they find or fix the error in a sentence. After warming up their mind to the grammar concept being taught, explicitly identifying the concept, and giving them some word lists, these practical exercises should be easy for children and should give them a chance to apply their newly learned skill. This is indeed another benefit of the Spot the Difference Grammar method. Before giving a lesson on, say, capitalizing people's names, we make sure that children know exactly what we are referring to. You would be amazed, but some children, even those who have been taught it, don't see the difference between upper and lower case letters. To them, functionally, "cat" and "Cat" read the same. When we make sure they have found the difference and then go on to explain the grammar concept, we know that they are clear about what we are talking about.

These practical exercises where they find or fix the errors in sentences otherwise also follow along children's learning cycle, where, after building knowledge and playing around with it, they apply their new skill to a real situation. I wanted to add these supplemental lessons such as to "clinch" the ideas in children's minds. To commit something to memory, you can't just learn something, you also have to use it. I did find that the exercises seemed to cement the grammar concepts that children learned. I would watch as children would spontaneously start to correct the grammar around them when they saw that it was incorrect.

A section for review

Finally, in alignment with the "Self-Reflective" stage of children's natural learning cycle, I added, at the end of the book, Spot the Difference activities where several grammar concepts are mixed together. There are no supplementary exercises with these. They are meant solely for review. Hopefully students can look back on all they learned and feel confident in what they have accomplished.

Topics covered

The topics covered in this Level 1 of Spot the Difference Grammar are some spelling and letter recognition, all basic punctuation and capitalization, and all eight basic parts of speech. The lessons are independent of each other, which is to say you can start with any lesson you want, but they do build on each other. The lessons are numbered and in general start with the easiest lessons and progress to harder ones. If you feel the first lessons are too easy for your child, you might look down the list until you find lessons that you feel are at your child's level. Section 1 is Spelling and Letter Recognition. Section 2 is Punctuation and Capitalization. Section 3 is Parts of Speech, and Section 4 is Review. I personally do not think children can get enough grammar practice—the subject is challenging to conquer—and I don't really recommend skipping over the first lessons. Even precocious children seem to enjoy the "easy" lessons. I have been told that even language-gifted children can struggle (in a good way) with Section 3 and happily learn new things. Below are my reasons for including certain subject matter, including "easy" things.

Spelling and Letter Recognition

This program is not a spelling program. However, I included some spelling lessons so as to do what this program does best, which is to show how something comes across when it is incorrect in a sentence, which is that it can cause confusion. Spelling words correctly is, as such, important! I otherwise only do enough spelling lessons as to cover each vowel.

I also include a little bit of letter recognition for the same reason. You would be amazed but even if they are fluent readers, children in 1st, 2nd, and even 3rd grade might not see why "h" and "n" are different. Why does it matter that the one line is just a bit bigger? This program easily shows that it's an entirely new letter and thus makes an entirely new word when read in a sentence. At any rate, it can give some needed review for some kids. Keep in mind that just because they are taught something, it doesn't mean that all children have retained it or don't have any other questions about it. Spot the Difference Grammar can help fill in unknown learning gaps.

Punctuation and Capitalization

For basic punctuation, I include almost every type of punctuation mark (periods, commas, etc.) that are used in most people's daily writing. I also added punctuation lessons that I thought would be interesting to young children, such as the colon that they would see on digital clocks. In general, I have found children had the most difficulty spotting the differences in upper versus lower case letters. This is why punctuation comes first in this section and capitalization comes second.

Parts of Speech

In this Level 1 program, all eight basic parts of speech are covered in a basic way. These lessons are in Section 3. Some parents tell me their kids could do Sections 1 and 2 independently but needed help in Section 3. Parts of speech are an abstract concept. Some of the lessons in this section also require an adult to model something for a child, such as getting up "quickly" versus "slowly." I in general recommend you do the lessons with children, but you might be able to let them do a lot of them on their own. However, Section 3, due to its more abstract nature, might demand your involvement. I think you might find doing these lessons on parts of speech fun. I personally, as an adult, developed a deeper appreciation and understanding of grammar itself (which is technically parts of speech and how sentences are arranged) by developing and working through Section 3.

Common Core standards

I looked up to see if this program covered what is required in the Common Core standards. This program again doesn't cover all topics, such as spelling and spelling patterns. However, for the areas that it does cover, which is grammar, capitalization, and punctuation, this Level 1 program covers all of the standards for kindergarten, 1st grade, 2nd grade, and most of 3rd grade. There were some things at the 3rd grade level, such as abstract nouns, that I thought would be better at older ages. It is my experience that children can vary in their language skills by one or even two years, so having a span of 1st through 3rd grade should allow you to focus on the skills you feel your student needs.

Many of the requirements in the Common Core standards asked that students "use" the concepts. For instance, children in Grade 1 should be able to "use frequently occurring adjectives." Of the books on the market that are designed to be in alignment with Common Core standards, a lot of them do exactly this. A grammar concept will be taught and then students are asked to demonstrate that concept by writing a sentence. For instance, they might learn what an action verb is and then they are asked to write a paragraph with five action verbs. I found young children don't tend to like this kind of assignment. None of us write like this. We don't write to prove we know what a verb is. We write because we have something to say. It is also difficult to think of words out of the blue, such as coming up with five action verbs, just to show you know a grammar concept.

In the supplementary activities in Spot the Difference Grammar, on the other hand, children do "use" the grammar concepts, but in a way that, I think, makes more sense for children. For instance, after learning what a verb is, there is a sentence expansion activity which simply asks them, "A dog _____." And they are free to fill it in with whatever they want. They have thereby "used" a verb. There is ample thought that doing exercises like this, which have students playing around with words to build sentences in a free and creative way, a little bit like they wood blocks to build structures as toddlers, is great for building their writing skills. For more, see *The Writing Revolution* by Judith Hochman and Natalie Wexler, in which they "break the writing process down into manageable chunks" with various activities that focus on the sentence itself, indeed such as sentence expansion activities, such as you will see in this program.

Targeted age

I designed Level 1 of Spot the Difference specifically for children aged 6. Children at this age can be very literal about everything, even copying letters down to the exact style of font when asked to. It is a great age to learn a few punctuation, capitalization, and grammar concepts in a stark, black-and-white way. However, people have told me they have successfully used this program with children as young as 5. I otherwise think this program can be of benefit to children anywhere between ages 6-9, which is roughly 1st through 3rd grade. For some children in this age range, it might be their first introduction to basic grammar and punctuation. For others, it might provide some happy, pressure-free review of basic grammar concepts. However, I did design it primarily for children aged 6. I found children at this age couldn't handle finding differences in more than just a few sentences, which is why the Spot the Difference lessons themselves are on the shorter side. For the supplemental activities, I otherwise added as many activities as would fit on the page, as to satisfy language-gifted children's thirst for writing activities. Please keep this in mind that not all children will want to complete all of the supplemental activities.

This program can also be used for spot review with older children (literally any age). For older elementary children, if I noticed they were struggling to, say, put an apostrophe in between their contractions, I would print off the Spot the Difference lesson on contractions for them. It is a pressure-free way to remind them of the syntax rule. I was often astonished by the kinds of questions children would have after doing the simple Spot the Difference lessons, as they explained why they weren't sure when or why to use a particular grammar concept. What could be better than children asking questions about how and when to properly use grammar? Indeed, another advantage of these simple lessons is that they don't take much to explain. It is hard to explain that a verb "shows action, links the subject to another word, or helps another verb." However, when you do a simple Spot the Difference Grammar lesson illustrating the concept, it becomes easy to talk about what a "verb" is.

Font choice

As children at age 6 are particular about how letters are shaped, it was important to put thought into what font to use. I chose to use Arial font for the activities. I really wanted to use a font that children will likely come across in daily life, such as Arial, Calibri, or Times New Roman. Calibri is my preferred font. However, let me give *you* a spot the difference activity. Can you spot the difference between this "g" and this "g"? The first "g" is in Calibri font and the latter is in Arial font. Can you see why it would confuse children? The latter "g," in Arial font, is truer to the "g" that children are typically taught when they are first learning their letters. In this "g," the curve at the top of it opens to the left. The other "g" has the curve at the top opening to the right. For the sake of children's learning, we make a big deal about how "b" and "d" are different because the curve at the bottom of these letters goes in a different direction, but in the font styles they come across routinely, children are faced with a "g" or maybe a "g," which are totally different! It's no wonder they struggle!

The "g" in Times News Roman font, which is "g," has the same issue. As such, I chose Arial font. I wish Arial font had an "a" that looked more like the "a" that children typically learn, which looks more like "a." This "a" was made in with Comic Sans font, which is a purposely whimsical font style and not otherwise commonly used, so I didn't use it. Arial font is otherwise a common font that shapes letters as close to what children are formally taught when they learn letters, and so I Arial font.

How to use the program

As noted, the lessons are listed in general order from easy to hard. Otherwise, the program is pretty straightforward. Parents tell me kids take to it right away. Please don't pressure children into the exercises if they don't want to do them. Otherwise, please give them at least a moment or two to work through the activities. If they struggle after a bit, please step in. A great way to find any differences you are missing is to read the sentences out loud. I felt that these exercises were easy enough, so I didn't include an Answer Key but if this becomes a problem, please email me at helloamber@gmail.com, and I will rectify the situation. (Please tell me the exact lesson and issue, as well, so I can look into what else might be going on.)

In the digital copy of this program (presented in PDF or Microsoft Word format), you can print off the lessons as desired. Each lesson, again, has exactly two sheets to it, except Section 4, which is review, and only has one page per lesson. Some people have told me they liked to print it into a binder with the first page on the left and the second page on the right. In the paperback version of this book, I have the lessons printed such that the first part of the lesson is on the left side of the page and the second part is on the right side. If you have the Word version of the document, you can change the lessons to your liking. For instance, there is a lesson with a letter to a child from their mom, which illustrates how to format a letter. You can customize this to be addressed to your child before you print it off, otherwise keeping the lesson itself intact. Each lesson only takes about 5 minutes. I numbered the lessons so as to help you plan your week or even your year. In total, there are 65 lessons. They are easily done one-on-one with a child or with a whole classroom of children. You are free to print off the lessons for your household or class.

A final note

I believe this program is a great introductory course to basic grammar that will set a solid foundation. It might be the case that students don't come away knowing everything right away. For instance, even after doing the lesson they might not know that a colon, "introduces things, such as lists." In my opinion, it's a lot to ask young children to know all of this information, including all of the parts of speech or what all punctuation marks do, even by 3rd grade. (I needed a refresher on colons and semicolons as an adult!) However, although students might not totally know what a colon does, they might notice that a colon has "two dots!" and this, in and of itself, is a worthwhile lesson. Children are going to come away from any program with what their mind was ready to learn, and this is the way it will be for any program. However, you can always do the lesson again later. I otherwise watched as children became gradually more sophisticated in their understanding of language concepts as they worked through Spot the Difference Grammar. At first, they might struggle to even see that one letter is capitalized and another is not. Towards the end of the program, they would be talking plainly about how, "Holidays need to be capitalized!" Learning is a personal, layered process that cannot be rushed.

On a personal note, I am very excited to present this Spot the Difference Grammar program. My passion has always been to educate children. I feel this program can educate any child from any background, including disadvantaged ones, as the exercises are so clear, straightforward, and fun for children. I believe children can nearly work through the exercises on their own. However, I do think, especially at this Level 1 age, that a supportive adult who sits down with them to talk to them about the exercises will greatly benefit them. This adult does not need to be an expert in grammar. The exercises are so straight forward that any willing adult (or even teenager) can help any child. This is a simple, pressure-free, effective way to learn grammar, which should take on a life of its own!

I hope you have as much fun as I had teaching children some grammar in a way that they find delightful!

Sincerely,

Amber Domoradzki ("The Observant Mom")

Benefits of Spot the Difference Grammar

- Incorrectly writing things gives an appreciation for writing things correctly. Seeing words misspelled for instance shows how this can cause confusion. Sentences missing entire words become hilariously wrong. We write well so others can understand us.
- Spotting specific differences guarantees the child knows what you are referring to when you give subsequent lessons. Some children, for instance, might not recognize the difference between lower and upper case letters or, rather, why this matters. For the functional purpose of reading, they seem to be the same. When they have identified what the difference is, you can go on to teach a lesson on the concept, knowing they know exactly what you are talking about.
- Simply circling differences allows children's minds to focus on the lesson, without getting too caught up in other things, like the mechanics of holding a pencil. They can simply observe and learn.
- An observational approach is a powerful way to teach grammar. In this program, however, there is a control of error. Students know they have completed the activity when they have found all of the differences.
- You can do "spot reviews" with older children who need review of a particular grammar concept. The Spot the Difference activity makes it easy to start a conversation about any given grammar concept.
- Children feel "on top" of grammar, not that grammar is on top of them.
- Children find spotting differences fun!

Quick tips for getting started

- The Spot the Difference activities have two sets of sentences. The correctly formatted set of sentences is labeled **"Correct."** The incorrectly formatted set of sentences is labeled "**Incorrect**." Students find the differences between these two sets of sentences.
- It doesn't matter if students circle the error in the "Correct" or "Incorrect" section. Either should be seen as fine.
- The lessons are listed in general order of easy to hard. If some of them seem too easy for your child, you might scroll through the lessons until you find lessons at their level. The lessons cover material that is listed in kindergarten through 3rd grade Common Core standards.
- Each lesson has two pages. On the page immediately following the Spot the Difference lesson is a page that contains a short summary explaining the grammar concept just illustrated. There are also supplemental activities on this second page. Please see the supplemental activities as optional.
- This program is not primarily meant to be a writing program. While some kids love to write at young ages, others don't. For the supplementary writing activities, please let children verbally state their answer if they don't want to write it.
- Some of the supplemental activities require an adult to help the child, such as modeling what some words mean or supplying them with a book to see certain grammar concepts. Students can otherwise probably work on most lessons on their own. However, it is recommended that at Level 1, which is meant for children aged 6-9, that an adult (or even a teenager) do the lessons with them.
- Try not to help children unless they ask for help or clearly get stuck. Then, please help them. If you do get stuck, reading the "Incorrect" sentences out loud might help.
- For extra emphasis on the grammar lesson taught, after students have spotted the differences, try reading the "Correct" and then "Incorrect" set of sentences out loud and talking about what you notice.
- Some of the supplemental activities call for specific children's books, so as to see the author's stylistic choices. On the page that follows this is a list of children's books that will be recommended and what grammar concept they illustrate. These are just suggestions are provided for your convenience only.

Recommended children's books

These are books that will be recommended in the pages that follow. Each shows off a particular grammar concept well. You are free, however, to use any book you like. This list was put together solely for your convenience.

Grammar Concept	Books
Exclamation and question marks	- *There Is A Bird On Your Head!* by Mo Willems - *Waiting Is Not Easy!* by Mo Willems - *Go, Dog. Go!* by P.D. Eastman - *Green Eggs and Ham* by Dr. Seuss - *The Little Engine That Could* by Watty Piper
All upper case letters indicate shouting	- *There Is A Bird On Your Head!* by Mo Willems - *Let's Go for a Drive!* by Mo Willems - *Waiting Is Not Easy!* by Mo Willems - *Green Eggs and Ham* by Dr. Seuss
Italics emphasize words	- *Watch Me Throw the Ball!* by Mo Willems - *The Thank You Book* by Mo Willems - *Waiting Is Not Easy!* by Mo Willems
Quotation marks show someone is talking	- *The Very Busy Spider* by Eric Carle - *The Little Engine That Could* by Watty Piper - *Goodnight Moon* by Margaret Wise Brown - *Go, Dog. Go!* by P.D. Eastman

Thank you!

Thank you for choosing Spot the Difference Grammar! Parents have overwhelmingly told me how fun this program is for their children. If you wouldn't mind, I would be ever grateful for a review with a few notes about what you experienced with this program at your favorite book retailer. I am a self-published author, essentially a really small business, and your review helps other parents and educators know what this program is all about. Thank you in advance!!

Section 1
Spelling and Letter Recognition

1-Spot the Difference!

Spot the **1** difference.

Correct

>Please put this in the bag.

Incorrect

>Please put this in the bad.

Spot the Difference Grammar Level 1

Lesson
There is a difference between g and d.

Word Lists

These are some words that begin with "g."

geese
gorilla
grapes
go

These are some words that begin with "d."

duck
dark
day
dance

Find the errors.

Find the **2** errors.

There were gucks and deese in the pond.

2-Spot the Difference!

Spot the **1** difference.

Correct

    Let's go home!

Incorrect

    Let's go nome!

Lesson
There is a difference between h and n.

Word Lists

These are some words that begin with "h."

hat
home
hair
hi

These are some words that begin with "n."

no
nose
night
now

Find the errors.

Find the **2** errors.

It's time for me to say good hight, as I have to go nome.

3-Spot the Difference!

Spot the **1** difference.

Correct

>A bird was in its nest.

Incorrect

>A dird was in its nest.

Lesson
There is a difference between **b** and **d**.

Word Lists

These are some words that begin with "b."

bed
bear
bird
bake

These are some words that begin with "d."

dad
duck
day
down

Find the errors.

Find the **2** errors.

    I am going to lay bown on my pillow, as it's time to go to ded.

Spot the Difference Grammar Level 1

4-Spot the Difference!

Spot the **4** differences.

Correct

A cat scratched a mat while chasing a rat and a bat.

Incorrect

A cta scratched a amt while chasing a rta and a bt.

Lesson
You found some spelling errors!

Activity

Write the following words without looking at them or say out loud how to spell them:

cat _____

rat _____

mat _____

bat _____

Spot the Difference Grammar Level 1

5-Spot the Differences!

Spot the **3** differences.

Correct

I took my pet to the vet because it got caught in a net.

Incorrect

I took my ept to the vte because it got caught in a et.

Spot the Difference Grammar Level 1

Lesson
You found some spelling errors!

Activity

Write the following words without looking at them or say out loud how to spell them:

pet _____

vet _____

net _____

6-Spot the Difference!

Spot the **3** differences.

Correct

    I am going to dig next to the big pig.

Incorrect

    I am going to dgi next to the ibg pg.

Lesson
You found some spelling errors!

Activity

Write the following words without looking at them or say out loud how to spell them:

dig   _____

big   _____

pig   _____

Spot the Difference Grammar Level 1

7-Spot the Differences!

Spot the **3** differences.

Correct

    Hop to put the mop on pop.

Incorrect

    Hpo to put the pom on pp.

Lesson
You found some spelling errors!

Activity

Write the following words without looking at them or say out loud how to spell them:

hop _____

mop _____

pop _____

8-Spot the Differences!

Spot the **3** differences.

Correct

Run and have some fun in the sun.

Incorrect

Rnu and have some fn in the usn.

Lesson
You found some spelling errors!

Activity

Write the following words without looking at them or say out loud how to spell them:

run   _____

fun   _____

sun   _____

Spot the Difference Grammar Level 1

Section 2
Punctuation and Capitalization

9-Spot the Differences!

Spot the **3** differences.

Correct

> Henry is funny.
>
> Where are you going?
>
> Watch me jump!

Incorrect

> Henry is funny
>
> Where are you going
>
> Watch me jump

Lesson
Every sentence needs to end with a punctuation mark.

Punctuation Marks

The three types of punctuation marks that can end a sentence are periods, exclamation marks, and question marks. They look like this:

Ending punctuation marks	What it looks like	What it does
Period	.	Signals the end of a complete sentence
Question mark	?	Shows that a question is being asked
Exclamation mark	!	Shows that very strong feeling is being expressed

Activity

Say the following sentences using different body language for each.

- I'm going to the beach.
- I'm going to the beach?
- I'm going to the beach!!!

Activity

Read a children's book that has exclamation and/or question marks in it. Use exaggerated bodily gestures based on the ending punctuation mark.

Recommendations:

- *There Is A Bird On Your Head!* by Mo Willems
- *Waiting Is Not Easy!* by Mo Willems
- *Go, Dog. Go!* by P.D. Eastman
- *Green Eggs and Ham* by Dr. Seuss
- *The Little Engine That Could* by Watty Piper

10-Spot the Differences!

Spot the **3** differences.

Correct

> Saturn is such a cool planet. It is famous for its rings. It is the second biggest planet.

Incorrect

> Saturn is such a cool planet It is famous for its rings It is the second biggest planet

Lesson
You just found some periods! We need periods because they finish a thought.

Activity

Try reading the "Incorrect" set of sentences but never pause after each sentence as there is no period. The sentences run on.

Activity

Which sentence is correct?

> The Great Red spot on Jupiter is a storm that has been raging for hundreds of years.

> The Great Red spot on Jupiter is a storm that has been raging for hundreds of years

Fix the errors.

Fix the **2** errors.

> Jupiter is huge

> Jupiter is twice the size of all other planets combined

11-Spot the Differences!

Spot the **2** differences.

Correct

The three planets closest to the sun are Mercury, Venus, and Earth.

Incorrect

The three planets closest to the sun are Mercury Venus and Earth.

Lesson
You just found some commas! Commas look like this **,** Commas (**,**) help us separate items in a list.

Finish the sentences.

My three favorite foods are _____ , _____ , and _____.

My three favorite numbers are _____ , _____ , and _____.

My three favorite colors are _____ , _____ , and _____.

Fix the errors.

Fix the 2 errors.

Please get me some apples grapes and bananas.

Spot the Difference Grammar Level 1

12-Spot the Difference!

Spot the **1** difference.

Correct

Stop eating Emily's cookies.

Incorrect

Stop eating Emilys cookies.

Lesson
You found an apostrophe! An apostrophe looks like this '
Apostrophes help us show possession. When we write "Emily's cookies," it means the cookies are Emily's. Without the apostrophe, it just seems like there are lots of Emilys!

Examples

These are examples of apostrophes showing possession.

Jacob's phone
Victoria's computer
Holly's house

Activity

Which sentence is correct?

    This is my brother's toy.

    This is my brothers toy.

Fix the error.

Find and fix the **1** error.

    We are going to my friend s house.

13-Spot the Differences!

Spot the **4** differences.

Correct

I'm at home. I'm playing a game on my computer with my sister. She's helping me win. Later, I'll take a bath.

Incorrect

I m at home. I m playing a game on my computer with my sister. She s helping me win. Later, I ll take a bath.

Lesson
You just found some contractions! Contractions "smoosh" words together. They shorten words and make them sound more casual.

Common contractions

Here are some examples of common contractions.

Full word/s	Contraction
do not	don't
cannot	can't
I am	I'm
I will	I'll
he is	he's
she is	she's
you are	you're
it is	it's
who is	who's

Activity

Read the paragraph together but expand the contractions into full words.

> I'm at home. I'm playing a game on my computer with my sister. She's helping me win. Later, I'll take a bath.

Find the error.

Fix the **1** error.

> I m going to my friend's house.

Spot the Difference Grammar Level 1

14-Spot the Differences!

Spot the **2** differences.

Correct

At the store we need two things: bread and milk.

We need to bring three things to the pool: a towel, a bathing suit, and water.

Incorrect

At the store we need two things; bread and milk.

We need to bring three things to the pool   a towel, a bathing suit, and water.

Lesson
You just found a colon! A colon has two dots. It looks like this :
Colons help us introduce things, such as lists.

Activity

Which sentence is correct?

    I have to pack two things in my backpack: pencils and books.

    I have to pack two things in my backpack; pencils and books.

Find the error.

Find the **1** error.

    Please get the following two things for dinner; steak and potatoes.

15-Spot the Difference!

Spot the **1** difference.

Correct

Lessons start at 2:00.

Incorrect

Lessons start at 200.

Lesson
A colon helps us separate hours and minutes when telling time.

Activity

Which sentence is correct?

>Soccer practice starts at 430.

>Soccer practice starts at 4:30.

Fix the error.

Fix the **1** error.

>I woke up today at 7 30.

16-Spot the Difference!

Spot the **1** difference.

Correct

    My sister won an award (yay!).

Incorrect

    My sister won an award yay! .

Lesson
You just found a pair of parentheses! Parentheses add extra information to a sentence.

Fix the errors.

Add the two matching parentheses to fix this sentence.

We're going to the museum   hooray!   .

17-Spot the Differences!

Spot the **6** differences.

Correct

"Let's go outside," said the oldest boy.

The girl then yelled, "Last one to the door is a rotten egg!"

"Wait for me!" said the six-year-old boy.

Incorrect

Let's go outside, said the oldest boy.

The girl then yelled, Last one to the door is a rotten egg!

Wait for me! said the six-year-old boy.

Lesson
You just found some quotation marks! We use quotation marks to show what a person said.

Activity Idea

Find children's books that have quotation marks that indicate a person is talking and read it with the students. Here are some suggestions.

- *The Very Busy Spider* by Eric Carle
- *The Little Engine That Could* by Watty Piper
- *Goodnight Moon* by Margaret Wise Brown
- *Go, Dog. Go!* by P.D. Eastman

Fix the errors.

Add the two quotation marks to this sentence showing the part that John said.

John joked, Did you hear the one about World War Pun?

18-Spot the Difference!

Spot the **1** difference.

Correct

My tablet is 75% charged.

Incorrect

My tablet is 75 charged.

Lesson
You just found a percent sign! A percent sign looks like this **%** Percents tell us how full something is or how much of something is left.

Activity

Find a % sign on a keyboard.

Fix the error.

Fix the **1** error.

    I am going to give 100   effort today.

19-Spot the Differences!

Spot the **2** differences.

Correct

      Monkeys live in jungles.

      Beavers build dams.

Incorrect

      monkeys live in jungles.

      beavers build dams.

Lesson
We capitalize the first word of every sentence! Capitalizing a word means we use an upper case letter and not a lower case letter for the first letter in the word.

Upper and Lower Case Letters

These are all the upper and lower case letters in the English alphabet.

Upper	A	B	C	D	E	F	G	H	I	J	K	L	M
Lower	a	b	c	d	e	f	g	h	i	j	k	l	m

Upper	N	O	P	Q	R	S	T	U	V	W	X	Y	Z
Lower	n	o	p	q	r	s	t	u	v	w	x	y	z

Activity

Which sentence is correct?

    raccoons have five toes on their front and back paws.

    Raccoons have five toes on their front and back paws.

Find the error.

Find the **1** error in this sentence.

    gorillas can weigh up to 500 pounds.

Spot the Difference Grammar Level 1

20-Spot the Differences!

Spot the **7** differences.

Correct

On Monday I ate one apple.

On Tuesday I ate two bananas.

On Wednesday I ate three blueberries.

On Thursday I ate four grapes.

On Friday I ate five oranges.

On Saturday I ate six strawberries.

And on Sunday I ate seven watermelons.

Incorrect

On monday I ate one apple.

On tuesday I ate two bananas.

On wednesday I ate three blueberries.

On thursday I ate four grapes.

On friday I ate five oranges.

On saturday I ate six strawberries.

And on sunday I ate seven watermelons.

Lesson
We capitalize the days of the week!

Days of the Week

These are the days of the week in order.

Days of the week	
1	Sunday
2	Monday
3	Tuesday
4	Wednesday
5	Thursday
6	Friday
7	Saturday

Activity

Finish these sentences.

The first day of the week is _____.

My favorite day of the week is _____.

Find the error!

Find the **1** error.

On thursday I have soccer practice.

Spot the Difference Grammar Level 1

21-Spot the Differences!

Spot the **2** differences.

Correct

Christmas is on December 25.

Incorrect

christmas is on december 25.

Lesson
We capitalize months and holidays.

Months and Holidays

These are the months of the year and some holidays in those months.

	Month	Holidays
1	January	New Year's Day
2	February	Valentine's Day
3	March	St. Patrick's Day
4	April	Easter (*sometimes Easter is in March)
5	May	Memorial Day (U.S. only)
6	June	
7	July	Independence Day (U.S. only)
8	August	
9	September	Labor Day (U.S. only)
10	October	Halloween
11	November	Thanksgiving (U.S. only)
12	December	Christmas

Activity

Finish these sentences.

The first holiday of the year is _____.

My favorite holiday is _____.

Find the error.

Find the **1** error.

halloween is celebrated in October.

22-Spot the Difference!

Spot the **1** difference.

Correct

The Emancipation Proclamation was signed on January 1, 1863.

Incorrect

The Emancipation Proclamation was signed on January 1 1863.

Lesson
There needs to be a comma between the day and year when writing a date.

Formatting a date

This is how to format a date.

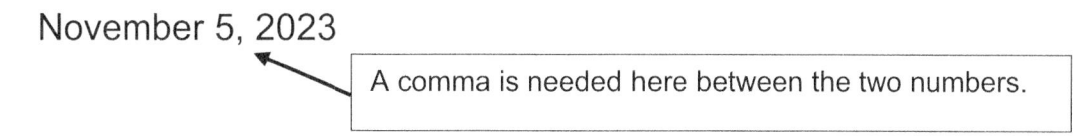

November 5, 2023

A comma is needed here between the two numbers.

Months

To help students spell them, here is a list of all the months.

January	February	March	April	May	June
July	August	September	October	November	December

Finish the sentence.

Please include the month, day, and year you were born.

I was born on _____.

Activity

Add the appropriate commas to these **3** dates.

September 5 2022

May 3 2014

November 29 1982

Spot the Difference Grammar Level 1

23-Spot the Difference!

Find the **2** differences.

Correct

      Clifford and I started home.

      I'm very good at doing math.

Incorrect

      Clifford and i started home.

      i'm very good at doing math.

Lesson
We always capitalize the word "I."
This means we use an upper case I and not a lower case i.

Find the errors!

Find the **2** errors.

    Today i am going to a museum. i'm very excited.

24-Spot the Differences!

Can you spot the **3** differences?

Correct

    Liam is funny.

    I wonder where Olivia is.

    Let's go pick up Sophia at acting class.

Incorrect

    liam is funny.

    I wonder where olivia is.

    Let's go pick up sophia at acting class.

Lesson
We capitalize the first letter of people's names!

Finish the sentences.

Be sure to capitalize the first letter of the names you write.

My name is _____.

My mom's name is _____.

My dad's name is _____.

Find the error.

Find the 1 error.

samantha is my best friend.

25-Spot the Differences!

Can you spot the **4** differences?

Correct

Ohio is a state in the United States of America.

Incorrect

ohio is a state in the united states of america.

Lesson

We capitalize the names of places!

Names of places

These are some examples of the names of places, including cities, countries, and landmarks. These are always capitalized.

Cities	Countries	Landmarks
• Atlanta • Boston • Chicago • Detroit • Hong Kong • Houston • London • Los Angeles • Melbourne • New York City • Paris • Singapore • Sydney • Tokyo • Toronto • Washington, D.C.	• Australia • Brazil • Canada • China • Egypt • France • India • Italy • Norway • Romania • Russia • South Africa • Sweden • United Kingdom • United States of America	• Colosseum • Eiffel Tower • Empire State Building • Golden Gate Bridge • Grand Canyon • Great Wall of China • Leaning Tower of Pisa • Statue of Liberty • Stonehenge • Taj Mahal • The White House

Activity

Which sentence is correct?

The Taj Mahal is in india.

The Taj Mahal is in India.

Find the error.

Find the **1** error.

Paris is in france.

Spot the Difference Grammar Level 1

26-Spot the Differences!

Spot the **2** differences.

Correct

> NATO stands for North Atlantic Treaty Organization.
>
> NASA stands for the National Aeronautics and Space Association.

Incorrect

> nato stands for North Atlantic Treaty Organization.
>
> nasa stands for the National Aeronautics and Space Association.

Lesson
You just found some acronyms! We always use all upper case letters for acronyms.

Examples of Acronyms

An acronym is an abbreviation using the first letter of each word of a phrase such that the result is a pronounceable word. Here are some examples of acronyms.

Acronym	Stands for
ASAP	As Soon As Possible
PIN	Personal Identification Number
POTUS	President of the United States
AWOL	Absent Without Leave

Examples of Abbreviations

Abbreviations combine the first letters of each word of a phrase, but you say the individual letters of the resulting word. Abbreviations are not always capitalized but can be. Here are some common abbreviations.

Abbreviation	Stands for
FBI	Federal Bureau of Investigation
BRB	Be Right Back
FYI	For Your Information
DIY	Do It Yourself
SMH	Shaking My Head
AFK	Away From Keyboard
BTW	By The Way
IDK	I Don't Know

Find the error.

Find the **1** error.

"fbi, open up!"

Spot the Difference Grammar Level 1

27-Spot the Difference!

What is the main difference between Option 1 and Option 2?

Option 1

Somewhere else.

Option 2

SOMEWHERE ELSE.

Lesson
In Option 2, the words are all in all upper case letters. Writing words in all upper case letters means someone is shouting or speaking very loudly.

All Upper Case Letters

These are some examples where words are not in all upper case letters and then when they are. If words are in all upper case letters, it indicates shouting.

Not all upper case letters	All upper case letters
Go away.	GO AWAY.
No.	NO.
Why?	WHY?

Activity

Read a children's book where words are capitalized. Shout or speak loudly when the words are capitalized.

Suggested books:

- *There Is A Bird On Your Head!* by Mo Willems
- *Let's Go for a Drive!* by Mo Willems
- *Waiting Is Not Easy!* by Mo Willems
- *Green Eggs and Ham* by Dr. Seuss

28-Spot the Difference!

Spot the **1** difference.

Option 1

It takes skill and practice.

Option 2

It takes skill *and* practice.

Lesson
You just found an italicized word! Deciding to italicize a word is not correct or incorrect. It is up to the writer to italicize a word or not. Italicizing a word adds emphasis to a word.

Italics

These are some examples of words in regular font and then in italics font.

Regular font	**In italics**
Thanking	*Thanking*
Everyone	*Everyone*
Important	*Important*

Activity

Read a child's book with italics in it, emphasizing words when they are italicized.

Some suggestions:

- *Watch Me Throw the Ball!* by Mo Willems
- *The Thank You Book* by Mo Willems
- *Waiting Is Not Easy!* by Mo Willems

29-Spot the Differences!

Spot the **4** differences.

Correct

Dear Brooklyn,

It is such a joy to be your mom. I love to hear you laugh. Great job winning the soccer challenge last night!

Love,

Mom

Incorrect

dear Brooklyn

It is such a joy to be your mom. I love to hear you laugh. Great job winning the soccer challenge last night!

love

Mom

Lesson
Above is how to format a letter. In it, we capitalize the letter greeting and closing, and we put a comma after the letter greeting and closing.

How to format a letter

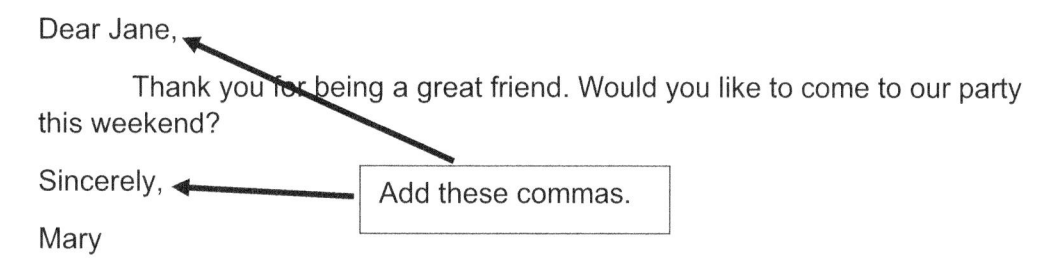

Dear Jane,

Thank you for being a great friend. Would you like to come to our party this weekend?

Sincerely,

Mary

Add these commas.

Activity

Write a letter to someone you know and send it in the mail.

Find the errors.

Find the **4** errors in this letter.

dear Santa

I've been a great kid this year. I hope to get some presents.

love

Emma

30-Spot the Differences!

Spot the **4** differences.

Correct

    Santa Claus

    123 Reindeer St.

    North Pole, AK 12345

Incorrect

    santa claus

    123 reindeer St.

    North Pole AK 12345

Lesson
You just learned how to format a United States address!

How to Address an Envelope

These are the parts of an address on an envelope.

First Name Last Name

Street Address

City, State Abbreviation Zip Code

A comma must be between the city and state abbreviation in an address.

State Abbreviations

Here is a list of the abbreviations for states, territories, and districts in the United States.

Alabama	AL	Illinois	IL	Montana	MT	Puerto Rico	PR
Alaska	AK	Indiana	IN	Nebraska	NE	Rhode Island	RI
Arizona	AZ	Iowa	IA	Nevada	NV	South Carolina	SC
Arkansas	AR	Kansas	KS	New Hampshire	NH	South Dakota	SD
California	CA	Kentucky	KY	New Jersey	NJ	Tennessee	TN
Colorado	CO	Louisiana	LA	New Mexico	NM	Texas	TX
Connecticut	CT	Maine	ME	New York	NY	Utah	UT
Delaware	DE	Maryland	MD	North Carolina	NC	Vermont	VT
District of Columbia	DC	Massachusetts	MA	North Dakota	ND	Virginia	VA
Florida	FL	Michigan	MI	Ohio	OH	Washington	WA
Georgia	GA	Minnesota	MN	Oklahoma	OK	West Virginia	WV
Hawaii	HI	Mississippi	MS	Oregon	OR	Wisconsin	WI
Idaho	ID	Missouri	MO	Pennsylvania	PA	Wyoming	WY

Fix the Errors!

Fix the **2** errors in this address. (Address is made up.)

Jane Doe

567 burgreen St.

Chicago IL 54382

Spot the Difference Grammar Level 1

Section 3
Parts of Speech

31-Spot the Difference!

Spot the **1** difference.

Correct

    The bird chirped.

Incorrect

        chirped.

Lesson
You just found the subject of a sentence! A proper sentence needs two things: who or what it's about (the subject) and what they are or are doing (the verb). The incorrect sentence doesn't tell us what chirped! This sentence is missing a subject.

Activity

Explain to students that a sentence needs two parts: who or what it's about and what they are or are doing. Then give some words with what something is doing but no subject. Some examples are "laughed" or "cooked." Have fun with this!

Complete the sentences.

_____ meowed.

_____ barked.

_____ neighed.

_____ hopped.

_____ flew.

_____ swam.

Spot the Difference Grammar Level 1

32-Spot the Differences!

Spot the **4** differences.

Correct

    The lion roars.

    The cat meows.

    The horse neighs.

    The sheep bleats.

Incorrect

    The lion.

    The cat.

    The horse.

    The sheep.

Lesson
You just found some verbs! Verbs help us show action. Every sentence needs two things: a subject and a verb. We need to know who or what the sentence is about and what about them. The "Incorrect" sentences don't tell us anything about the lion, cat, horse, or sheep!

Activity

Explain that a proper sentence needs both who or what we are talking about and what they are doing or are. Simply state objects and ask if it's a complete sentence. For instance, simply say "shirt" or "table." Have fun with it!

Complete the following sentences.

The dog _____.

The monkey _____.

The goat _____.

The mouse _____.

I _____.

My mom _____.

My dad _____.

33-Spot the Differences!

Spot the **4** differences.

Correct

> Grass is green.
>
> Ice is cold.
>
> Cheetahs are fast.
>
> Whales are HUGE!

Incorrect

> Grass green.
>
> Ice cold.
>
> Cheetahs fast.
>
> Whales HUGE!

Lesson

You just found some more verbs! Verbs also help us show a state of being. Words like "is" and "are" help tell us about what something is.

Complete the sentences.

Complete the following sentences. Fill them in with what you want. There are no right or wrong answers to these!

The sun is _____.

The sky is _____.

The ocean is _____.

Trees are _____.

Winter is _____.

Summer is _____.

34-Spot the Differences!

Spot the **4** differences.

Correct

There are lots of fast animals in Africa. Ostriches can reach speeds of 45 miles per hour. Lions can reach a top speed of 50 miles per hour. But the fastest land animal of all is the cheetah. Cheetahs can run up to 75 miles per hour!

Incorrect

There are lots of fast animal in Africa. Ostrich can reach speeds of 45 miles per hour. Lion can reach a top speed of 50 miles per hour. But the fastest land animal of all is the cheetah. Cheetah can run up to 75 miles per hour!

Spot the Difference Grammar Level 1

Lesson
You just found some plural nouns! Singular nouns show us that there is one thing. Plural nouns show that there is more than one thing.

Singular versus Plural Nouns

Most nouns become plural by adding an "s."

lion	lions
book	books

Some nouns become plural by adding "es."

ostrich	ostriches
tomato	tomatoes

Some are **irregular** plural nouns.

child	children
man	men
woman	women
foot	feet
tooth	teeth

Some plural nouns are the same as their singular noun.

fish	fish
sheep	sheep

Finish the sentence.

Finish this sentence.

The dentist is going to check all of my _____.

35-Spot the Differences!

Spot the **5** differences.

Correct

A schoolteacher waited for her class to sit down and be quiet.

An entire galaxy of stars twinkled in the night.

She shuffled the deck of cards.

Daddy gave mommy a bouquet of flowers.

A fleet of ships attacked England.

Incorrect

A schoolteacher waited for her army to sit down and be quiet.

An entire herd of stars twinkled in the night.

She shuffled the gaggle of cards.

Daddy gave mommy a deck of flowers.

A forest of ships attacked England.

Lesson
You just found some collective nouns! Collective nouns describe a group of something.

Collective Nouns

These are some examples of collective nouns and what they describe.

Collective noun	Group of:
forest	trees
galaxy	stars
gaggle	geese
flock	sheep
harvest	recently picked vegetables
herd	cows
pack	wolves
deck	cards
bouquet	flowers
school	fish
class	students
team	players
crowd	people who are close together
army	soldiers
batch	cookies

Complete the sentences.

A _____ of wolves were heard howling in the night.

My baseball _____ won last night.

36-Spot the Differences!

Spot the **2** differences.

Option 1

Put the pencil on the table.

Option 2

Put the thing on the thing.

Lesson

You found some specific nouns! Specific nouns tell us more than generic nouns. Using a generic noun isn't right or wrong but when we aren't specific when we should be, it can cause confusion.

Activity

Ask students to go get something, using generic language at first and getting more specific. This is a suggested sequence,

1. Please get me the thing.
2. Oh, you know, the toy.
3. Oh, please get me your stuffed animal!

Spot the Difference Grammar Level 1

37-Spot the Differences!

Spot the **3** differences.

Option 1

Giraffes are the tallest animals on earth. They can be as tall as 18 feet. They can weigh up to 4,200 pounds! They like to eat leaves.

Option 2

Giraffes are the tallest animals on earth. Giraffes can be as tall as 18 feet. Giraffes can weigh up to 4,200 pounds! Giraffes like to eat leaves.

Lesson
You just found some pronouns! Pronouns are words like "he," "she," "they," and "them," which take the place of a noun. It's not wrong or right to use pronouns but without them the text gets repetitive.

Examples of pronouns

These are some examples of pronouns and what they do.

I	used when referring to yourself.
You	used when referring to the person you're addressing.
He	used when referring to a third person of masculine gender.
She	used when referring to a third person of feminine gender.
It	used when referring to a thing, place, or animal.
We	used when referring to a group of people that you're a part of.
You	used when referring to the group of people you're addressing.
They	used when referring to a group of people you're not a part of.

Find the pronouns

Can you circle the **2** pronouns?

My dad loves to cook. He cooked for us last night. He made us spaghetti!

Can you circle the **2** pronouns?

My sister is great at drawing. Last night she drew a really cool fish! Today she is going to draw a cat.

38-Spot the Differences!

Spot the **2** differences.

Correct

She threw the ball.

She tossed the ball.

Incorrect

She   the ball.

She   the ball.

Lesson
You found some more verbs! Different verbs describe different actions. Using a specific verb helps us describe exactly how something moves.

Activity

Have fun showing the different ways you can move a ball. You can:

- Throw a ball.
- Hurl a ball.
- Toss a ball.
- Roll a ball.
- Drop a ball.

Activity

Have fun showing how people can move. We can:

- Run
- Walk
- Hop
- Skip
- Twirl

Activity

Circle the word that describes how Rebecca moved.

Rebecca skipped over to the swing.

39-Spot the Differences!

Spot the **3** differences.

Correct

They race. They relax. They eat.

Incorrect

They races. They relaxes. They eats.

Lesson
You found some plural verbs! Plural nouns need plural verbs. In general, plural verbs do **not** end in "s."

Singular versus Plural Nouns

Singular nouns refer to just one person, place, thing, or idea. Plural nouns refer to more than one person, place, thing, or idea.

Singular nouns	Plural nouns
cat	cats
dog	dogs
monkey	monkeys
I	we
Emma	Emma and Sam
Mom	Mom and Dad

Activity

Circle the verb that complements the plural nouns.

They (explore/explores) a new cave.

Emma and Sam (agrees/agree) to the rules of the game.

They (eats/eat) bread.

Find the errors.

Find the **2** errors.

The children are going to have a great day. First, they are going to plays on the playground. Then they are going to eats lunch. Finally, they will go home.

40-Spot the Differences!

Spot the **3** differences.

Correct

He races. He relaxes. He eats.

Incorrect

He race. He relax. He eat.

Lesson
You found some singular verbs! Singular nouns need singular verbs. In general, singular verbs end in "s."

Singular versus Plural Verbs

Singular verbs usually end in "s."

Singular verb	Plural verb
agrees	agree
explores	explore
bakes	bake
counts	count
enjoys	enjoy

Irregular singular versus plural verbs

Singular verb	Plural verb
is	are
does	do

Activity

Circle the right verb that complements the singular nouns.

She (use/uses) a spoon.

Henry (are/is) funny.

She (does/do) her homework.

Find the errors.

Find the **2** errors.

What a delightful day. We got to see a cat. He had a long tail and was black and white. He are super playful. He enjoy playing with string. I hope we get to see him again!

Spot the Difference Grammar Level 1

41-Spot the Difference!

Spot the **1** difference.

Correct

>Yesterday was a really great day. We went to a park. I played in the sandbox. We also had a picnic. I had so much fun!

Incorrect

>Yesterday was a really great day. We went to a park. I play in the sandbox. We also had a picnic. I had so much fun!

Lesson
Verbs can help us describe something that happened in the past. These verbs often end in "d" or "ed."

Present versus Past Verbs

These are some examples of verbs in their present and past tense.

Present verb	Past verb
talk	talked
walk	walked
play	played
open	opened
show	showed
love	loved

Activity

Which of these sentences describe something the bunny did in the **past**?

The bunny hopped through the field.

The bunny hops through the field

Fix the paragraph.

Find the **1** error.

I had a great time at grandma's house yesterday. We play Go Fish together. I can't wait to go back.

Spot the Difference Grammar Level 1

42-Spot the Difference!

Spot the **1** difference.

Correct

    I brought a pencil with me.

Incorrect

    I bringed a pencil with me.

Lesson

Most (regular) verbs become past tense by adding "-ed." But some are irregular and don't follow this convention.

Irregular Verbs

These are some examples of incorrect and correct irregular verbs.

Verb	Incorrect Past Tense	Correct Past Tense
bring	bringed	brought
think	thinked	thought
make	maked	made
bite	bited	bit
know	knowed	knew

Activity

Which of these sentences is correct?

    I maked a card.

    I made a card.

Find the error!

Find the **1** error.

    I thinked really hard about that problem.

Spot the Difference Grammar Level 1

43-Spot the Difference!

Spot the **1** difference.

Correct

Tomorrow is going to be a great day. We will swim in the pool!

Incorrect

Tomorrow is going to be a great day. We swim in the pool!

Lesson
Verbs can help us describe something that will happen in the future. Verbs in future tense often follow the formula "will" + [verb].

Present versus Future Tense Verbs

These are some examples of verbs in their present and future tense.

Present verb	Future verb
talk	will talk
walk	will walk
play	will play
open	will open
eat	will eat

Activity

Which of these sentences describe something that will happen in the **future**?

> We opened our presents.

> We will open our presents.

Find the error.

Find the **1** error.

> I can't wait to go to the store tomorrow. We buy some toys!

44-Spot the Differences!

Spot the **2** differences.

Correct

> I like to add salt and pepper to my vegetables.

> On Saturday mornings, we make bacon and eggs.

Incorrect

> I like to add salt pepper to my vegetables.

> On Saturday mornings, we make bacon eggs.

Lesson
You found the word "and"! We use "and" to make pairs.

Word List

These are some famous pairs joined by the word "and."

Famous pairs
apples and bananas
peas and carrots
peanut butter and jelly
oil and vinegar
forks and knives
cats and dogs

Activity

Without the "and" in the spot the difference activity, it reads as "bacon eggs." Ask your students what "bacon eggs" are.

Activity

Complete the sentences. Note: It's ok if children just say it.

My two favorite foods are _____.

My two favorite colors are _____.

45-Spot the Differences!

Spot the **2** differences.

Correct

    Do you like cats or dogs better?

    Do you want to use a fork or spoon?

Incorrect

    Do you like cats dogs better?

    Do you want use a fork spoon?

Lesson
You just found the word "or"! The word "or" indicates that a choice has to be made.

Activity

Have fun with some "Would you rather?" questions.

1. Would you rather be able to be invisible or be able to fly?
2. Would you rather have wings but never be able to touch the ground or be able to touch the ground but never have wings?
3. Would you rather fly to space or visit every country?
4. Would you rather it be really hot or really cold?
5. Would you rather fly like a bird or swim like a fish?

Activity

Invite students to ask you their own "Would you rather?" questions.

46-Spot the Differences!

Spot the **4** differences.

Correct

      Mars and Saturn are planets in our solar system.

      Would you rather visit Mars or Saturn?

      Saturn is a big planet but not the biggest.

      Saturn is huge yet it would float on water.

Incorrect

      Mars Saturn are planets in our solar system.

      Would you rather visit Mars Saturn?

      Saturn is a big planet   not the biggest.

      Saturn is huge   it would float on water.

Lesson
You just found some conjunctions! A "junction" is where two things meet. Similarly, conjunctions join words or ideas together in different yet specific ways.

Common conjunctions

This is a list of some of the most common conjunctions.

Common conjunctions
and
or
but
yet

Activity

Circle the word that is a conjunction in each of the following sentences. Only one word in each sentence will be circled.

    The child is both smart and strong.

    The child is strong but clumsy.

    He could choose soccer or dancing.

    She is tall yet fast.

Spot the Difference Grammar Level 1

47-Spot the Differences!

Can you spot the **2** differences?

Correct

      Let's eat a banana.

      Let's eat an apple.

Incorrect

      Let's eat an banana.

      Let's eat a apple.

Lesson
You just find some articles! Articles are words like "a," "an," and "the." They clarify who or what you are referring to.

Find the vowels.

Whether or not we use "a" or "an" depends on if the word following it makes a vowel or consonant sound. The letters **a, e, i. o,** and **u** are vowels. All the rest are consonants.

Can you circle the **5** vowels?

a	b	c	d	e	f	g	h	i	j	k	l	m
n	o	p	q	r	s	t	u	v	w	x	y	z

When to use "a" or "an"

Deciding between using "a" or "an" depends on the word immediately following it.

Examples of when to use "a"

Use "a" when the word that immediately follows it begins with a consonant sound.

    We are going to ride a **t**rain.

    We are going to buy a **c**ar.

    We petted a **d**og.

Examples of when to use "an"

Use "an" when the word that immediately follows it begins with a vowel sound.

    We are going to board an **a**irplane.

    We are going to crack an **e**gg.

    We need an **u**mbrella.

Note that "an" is used in front of words like "hour" because the "h" makes a vowel-like sound.

Activity

Choose if you would use "a" or "an."

    We saw (an/a) cat.

    We are going to (an/a) aquarium.

48-Spot the Differences!

Spot the **4** differences.

Correct

      Big dogs sometimes have small barks.

      Small dogs sometimes have big barks.

Incorrect

        dogs sometimes have   barks.

        dogs sometimes have   barks.

Lesson
You just found some adjectives! Adjectives help us modify nouns by making them more specific. By removing the adjectives, these sentences make no sense.

Common Adjectives

These are some common adjectives.

Common Adjectives	
big	small
thin	thick
dull	sharp
soft	hard
short	long
black	white
red	yellow
cold	hot
nice	mean

Activity

Take any object, such as a pencil or shirt, and describe it. Is it big? Hard? Soft? What color is it? Have students do this by themselves if they are capable or work with them.

Words to describe the object.

1. _____

2. _____

3. _____

4. _____

5. _____

49-Spot the Differences!

Spot the **2** differences.

Correct

Ann is fast at running. Tom is faster. Beth is the fastest.

Incorrect

Ann is fast at running. Tom is more faster. Beth is the most fastest.

Lesson
You found some more adjectives! Adjectives can also help us compare objects.

Comparative and Superlative Adjectives

These are some common comparative and superlative adjectives.

Adjective	Comparative	Superlative
loud	louder	loudest
quiet	quieter	quietest
fast	faster	fastest
high	higher	highest
tall	taller	tallest
big	bigger	biggest
small	smaller	smallest
good	better	best

Activity

Act out any of the above comparatives and superlatives. Emphasize again that we don't say for instance "more bigger" but just "bigger." Some suggestions:

- Talk loudly, louder, and then as loud as you can.
- Talk quietly, then quieter, then as quietly as you can.
- Run fast, faster, then as fast as you can.
- Line a few people up from tall to tallest.
- Arrange blocks from the smallest to biggest. Identify which are small, smaller and the smallest and then which are big, bigger, and the biggest.
- Write a letter from the alphabet pretty well, then a bit better, then as well as you possibly can.

Fix the error.

Cross out the word that isn't needed in this sentence.

Jupiter is the most biggest planet.

50-Spot the Differences!

Spot the **4** differences.

Correct

A mouse quietly scurries across the floor.

Hummingbirds feed hungrily on flower nectar.

The rabbit runs quickly away from the fox.

The bird sings sweetly.

Incorrect

A mouse quiet scurries across the floor.

Hummingbirds feed hungry on flower nectar.

The rabbit runs quick away from the fox.

The bird sings sweet.

Lesson

You found some adverbs! Adverbs help us describe how something is done. Adverbs often end in the letters -ly.

Activity

Demonstrate how you can do the following actions in the following ways. Model the actions for students and then have them do it.

Verb	Adverb
Walk	Slowly
	Quickly
	Backwards
	Aimlessly
	Boldly
Talk	Loudly
	Quietly
Get up	Immediately
	Slowly

Activity

Circle the word that tells us **how** Timmy walked.

Timmy walked quickly to his desk.

Circle the word that tells us **how** Caroline talked.

Caroline talked quietly to her friend.

51-Spot the Differences!

Spot the **3** differences.

Correct

We'll eat dinner later.

We've been practicing since this morning.

It rained all day.

Incorrect

We'll eat dinner lately.

We've been practicing since this .

It rained day.

Lesson
You found some more adverbs! Adverbs also help us describe *when* and *how long* something happened.

Activity

Have students do the following.

>Hop on one foot now.
>
>Hop on one foot for five seconds.
>
>Hop on one foot five seconds from now.
>
>Hop on one foot five seconds from now for five seconds.

Adverbs

Adverbs can also show us when or how long something happened.

Adverbs showing *when* something happened
now
earlier
later
yesterday
tomorrow

Adverbs showing *how long* something happened
for ten seconds
all day
since this morning

Activity

Circle the word in the sentence that tells us **when** something is going to happen.

>We are going to eat now.

52-Spot the Differences!

Spot the **3** differences.

Correct

    The kids are upstairs.

    We went indoors.

    He doesn't live here.

Incorrect

    The kids are .

    We went .

    He doesn't live .

Spot the Difference Grammar Level 1

Lesson
You found some more adverbs! Adverbs also help us describe *where* something happened.

Activity

Circle or say if the underlined word is showing how, when, or where to do something.

They played <u>upstairs</u>. (How, When, Where)

I listened <u>closely</u> to the teacher. (How, When, Where)

I am going to cook dinner <u>later</u>. (How, When, Where)

53-Spot the Differences!

Spot the **5** differences.

Correct

> Where did the ball go? Is it on the table? Is it under the sink? Is it in the bathroom? Is it between the couch cushions? Is it beside the shelf?

Incorrect

> Where did the ball go? Is it   the table? Is it   the sink? Is it the bathroom? Is it   the couch cushions? Is it   the shelf?

Lesson
You just found some prepositions! Prepositions help us explain where things are.

Activity

Let's listen to "The Prepositions Song" by Scratch Garden.

Prepositions Showing Where

These are some common prepositions showing where something is.

Common prepositions that show where something is
beneath
beside
between
in
in front of
inside
near
on
under

Fill in the following sentences.

The child is sitting _____ the chair.

The dog is _____ the table.

The tree is _____ the house.

Spot the Difference Grammar Level 1

54-Spot the Differences!

Spot the **2** differences.

Correct

>Oh my! What a day! I came home from school at 1:00 today! There was a blizzard! Who would think that it would snow in March in Ohio?

Incorrect

>Oh my! What a day! I came home from school   1:00 today! There was a blizzard! Who would think that it would snow   March in Ohio?

Spot the Difference Grammar Level 1

Lesson
You found some more prepositions! Prepositions also help us explain *when* things happened.

Prepositions of when

The words "in," "on," and "at" help us describe when something happened. Here are some examples of these prepositions with their prepositional phrases.

Prepositional phrases showing when something happened
in the morning
in January
in 2016
on Friday
on July 30
at 6:00
at night

Activity

In each sentence, circle the words that tell us when something happened.

In the morning, I ate breakfast.

I came home from school at 2:00.

On September 30, I am going camping.

Find the error.

Circle the **1** error.

I am going to grandma's house in 6:00.

Spot the Difference Grammar Level 1

55-Spot the Difference!

Spot the **1** difference.

Option 1

I fell down and hurt my knee. Ow!

Option 2

I fell down and hurt my knee.

Lesson
You found an interjection. Interjections are words like "Wow!" or "Ow!" It's not right or wrong to use an interjection, but they add emotion to what is written.

Common Interjections

This is a list of common interjections and what kind of emotion they express. Interjections are usually followed by an exclamation mark.

Pain	Displeasure	Pleasure	Congratulations	Fear
• Ow! • Ouch!	• Boo! • Ew! • Yuck!	• Yay! • Yippee!	• Cheers! • Congratulations!	• Eek! • Yikes!

Activity

Interjections are fun for kids. Ask them what their favorite is.

Find the word.

Find the **1** interjection.

My friend caught a frog and it peed on him. Yuck!

Section 4
Review

56-Spot the Differences!

Spot the **4** differences.

Correct

A black hole is a place in space where gravity pulls so much that even light cannot get out. Because no light can get out, you can't see black holes. Black holes are invisible!

Incorrect

A black hole is a place in space where gravity pulls so much that even light cannot get out Because no light can get out, you cant see black holes. Black hoels are invisible

57-Spot the Differences!

Spot the **3** differences.

Correct

> An eclipse happens when a planet or a moon gets in the way of the Sun's light. Here on Earth, we can experience two kinds of eclipses: solar eclipses and lunar eclipses.

Incorrect

> An eclipse happens when a planet or a moon gets in the way of the Suns light Here on Earth, we can experience two kinds of eclipses solar eclipses and lunar eclipses.

58-Spot the Differences!

Spot the **5** differences.

Correct

> There is no such thing as a picky grizzly bear. Grizzly bears eat a wide variety of food. This helps them live through many seasons. Some of the food items that grizzly bears eat are moose, deer, rodents, insects, birds, and fruit.

Incorrect

> There is no such thing as a picky grizzly bear. Grizzly bears eat a wide variety of food. This helps them live through many seasons. Some of the food items that grizzly bears eat are moose deer rodents insects birds and fruit.

59-Spot the Differences!

Spot the **4** differences.

Correct

> There are many things that certain animals can do that we can't. For instance, we can't regenerate body parts like the amphibious axolotl can. We can't run across water like the basilisk lizard can. And we can't sleep with one eye open like dolphins can. But wouldn't it be cool if we could?

Incorrect

> There are many things that certain animals can do that we cant. For instance, we cant regenerate body parts like the amphibious axolotl can. We can't run across water like the basilisk lizard can. And we can't sleep with one eye open like dolphins can. But wouldnt it be cool if we could

60-Spot the Differences!

Spot the **2** differences.

Correct

    Let's go see a play on Friday.

Incorrect

    let's go see a play on friday.

61-Spot the Differences!

Spot the **2** differences.

Correct

> The shepherd tended to his flock of sheep. His feet hurt after walking all day.

Incorrect

> The shepherd tended to his class of sheep. His foots hurt after walking all day.

62-Spot the Differences!

Spot the **2** differences.

Correct

> John F. Kennedy was the 35th president of the United States. He is famous for saying, "Ask not what your country can do for you. Ask what you can do for your country."

Incorrect

> John F. Kennedy was the 35th president of the United States. He is famous for saying, Ask not what your country can do for you. Ask what you can do for your country.

63-Spot the Differences!

Spot the **4** differences.

Correct

Many animals are capable of doing impressive things. A cheetah can run up to 70 miles per hour. A flea can jump 200 times its body length. Which would you rather do: run really fast or jump really high?

Incorrect

Many animals are capable of doing impressive things. A cheetah can runs up to 70 miles per hour. A flea can jumps 200 times its body length. Which would you rather do run really fast or jump really high

64-Spot the Differences!

Spot the **2** differences.

Correct

There is a famous saying, "An apple a day keeps the doctor away."

Incorrect

There is a famous saying, "A apple an day keeps the doctor away."

65-Spot the Differences!

Spot the **4** differences.

Correct

> Did you have fun spotting the differences between two sets of sentences? Do you know other children who might like it? Be sure to recommend Spot the Difference Grammar to your friends!

Incorrect

> Did you have fnu spotting the differences between two sets of sentences Do you know other children who might like it? Be sure to recommends Spot the Difference Grammar to your friends

Printed in Great Britain
by Amazon